Native Americans

The Comanche

Richard M. Gaines

ABDO Publishing Company

visit us at
www.abdopub.com

Published by ABDO Publishing Company, 4940 Viking Drive, Suite 622, Edina, Minnesota 55435. Copyright © 2000 Abdo Consulting Group, Inc., Pentagon Tower, P.O. Box 36036, Minneapolis, Minnesota 55435 USA. International copyrights reserved in all countries. No part of this book may be reproduced in any form without written permission from the publisher.

Published 2000
Printed in the United States of America
Second Printing 2002

Illustrator: David Kanietakeron Fadden
Interior Photos: Corbis (pgs. 4, 15, 27); Liz Pollard (pgs. 28, 29)
Editors: Bob Italia, Tamara L. Britton, Kate A. Furlong
Art Direction & Maps: Pat Laurel
Border Design: Carey Molter/MacLean & Tuminelly (Mpls.)

Library of Congress Cataloging-in-Publication Data

Gaines, Richard M., 1942-
     The Comanche / Richard M. Gaines.
         p. cm. -- (Native Americans)
     Includes bibliographical references and index.
     Summary: Presents a brief introduction to the Comanche Indians including information on their society, homes, food, clothing, crafts and life today.
     ISBN 1-57765-372-6
     1. Comanche Indians--Juvenile literature. [1. Comanche Indians. 2. Indians of North America--Southwest, New.] I. Title.

E99.IN3 G35 2000
979. 1'004972--dc21
                                                        99-059870

Special thanks to Liz Pollard of the American Indian Exposition for her generosity and assistance.

Contributing Editor: Barbara Gray, JD

Barbara Gray, JD (Kanatiyosh) is a member of the Mohawk Nation (Akwesasne), which is in New York State and Canada. Barbara earned her Juris Doctorate from Arizona State University College of Law in May of 1999. She is presently pursuing a Doctorate in Justice Studies that focuses on American Indian culture and issues at Arizona State University. When she finishes school, she will return home to the Mohawk Nation.

Illustrator: David Kanietakeron Fadden

David Kanietakeron Fadden is a member of the Akwesasne Mohawk Wolf Clan. His work has appeared in publications such as *Akwesasne Notes, Indian Time*, and the *Northeast Indian Quarterly*. Examples of his work have also appeared in various publications of the Six Nations Indian Museum in Onchiota, NY. His work has also appeared in "How The West Was Lost: Always The Enemy," produced by Gannett Production which appeared on the Discovery Channel. David's work has been exhibited in Albany, NY; the Lake Placid Center for the Arts; Centre Strathearn in Montreal, Quebec; North Country Community College in Saranac Lake, NY; Paul Smith's College in Paul Smiths, NY; and at the Unison Arts & Learning Center in New Paltz, NY.

Contents

Where They Lived

Before 1700, the Comanche were part of the large Northern Shoshone tribe. They lived in the mountains of Wyoming and Colorado.

Around 1705, the Comanche began to trade for horses with New Mexico's Pueblo tribe. The Comanche used these horses to travel to the plains of eastern Colorado and Kansas. There, they hunted buffalo.

The Comanche were fierce warriors and skilled horsemen. Soon, they pushed other tribes aside. They moved farther south into Oklahoma and Texas. Comanche lands were called the Comancheria.

The Comanche were most powerful in the early 1800s. The tribe had about 10,000 people.

The plains of Colorado, where the Comanche hunted buffalo

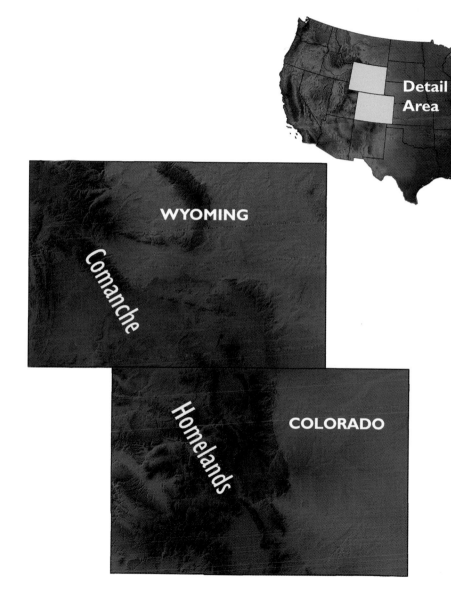

Detail
Area

WYOMING

Comanche

COLORADO

Homelands

The
Comanche
Homelands

Society

The Comanche tribe was made up of several large **bands**. A family could live with any Comanche band they chose. These Comanche bands all spoke the same language. They rarely fought with each other.

The Penateka, or "honey eaters," lived in central Texas. North of them lived the Nokoni, or "wanderers." The Kototeka, or "buffalo eaters," lived in Oklahoma. The Yamaparika, or "root eaters," lived in Kansas. The Quahadi, or "antelope eaters," lived in west Texas and New Mexico.

Each band had a chief, a war chief, and a peace chief. Each band followed the advice of the experienced peace chiefs, who were respected **elders**. They were wise, even-tempered, and generous. They possessed great knowledge of the land. Peace chiefs from different family camps often met in **council**. They helped solve the band's problems.

Comanche peace chief (left) and war chief

Homes

The Comanche moved often in search of buffalo, pecans, prickly pears, and other food. So, their tipis had to be simple to construct and easy to carry.

The Comanche fitted their horses with a **travois**. It carried heavy loads, including the tipi.

Long, wooden poles were used to make an upside-down cone frame of the tipi. The frame was covered with about 12 to 17 buffalo hides that had been sewn together. A Comanche woman could put one up in about fifteen minutes.

The tipi was about 15 feet (4.6 m) high. Its base was about 15 feet (4.6 m) across. In the summer, the buffalo hides near the base were rolled up. This allowed a cool breeze to pass through the tipi.

In the winter, furs were stacked up on the ground and a fire was built in the center of the tipi. Flaps in the top of the tipi allowed smoke to escape. Two long poles controlled the smoke flaps. When the flaps were open, the smoke escaped. If the weather was cold, the smoke flaps were closed to keep the tipi warm.

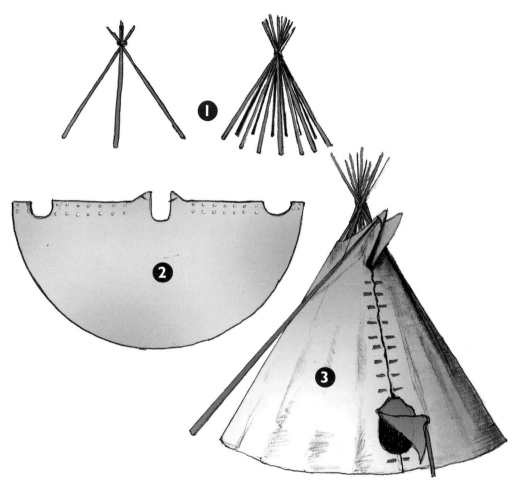

Tipi construction: 1. The pole frame 2. The buffalo-hide cover. 3. The finished tipi with door flap and smoke flap.

Food

When they lived in Wyoming and Colorado, the Comanche were hunter-gatherers. They hunted deer and elk. They did not plant crops. They gathered foods that grew naturally.

When the Comanche moved to Kansas and eastern Colorado, most of their food and supplies came from buffalo.

In the summer and fall, the entire **band** moved near the buffalo herds. Men on horseback surrounded a small herd. Then, they rode among the buffalo, shooting them with arrows. To do this, the hunters had to get close to the buffalo. This took great skill and courage.

Once a buffalo was killed, the men skinned it. They cut the meat and carried it back to camp.

The women prepared the meat. They hung it on drying racks. Then, the women and girls prepared the buffalo hides for **tanning**.

Buffalo horns were made into ladles and cups. **Sinew** was taken from the back of the buffalo. It was used for thread and bowstrings.

The stomach was prepared and then used to heat water. The stomach was propped up with sticks. Then, water and hot rocks were added. The hot rocks heated the water.

Comanche on a buffalo hunt

Clothing

Women often wore knee-length, deerskin skirts. They had **fringes** along the seams and **hemline**. A **poncho**-like top was worn with the dress. It was made from one skin. And it had a narrow opening for the head.

Men wore knee-length **breechcloths**. They were decorated with shells and long fringes. Thigh-length leggings were worn and tied below the knees.

Young girls wore a deerskin breechcloth. When they were around the age of 12, they wore buckskin dresses. Boys wore deerskin breechcloths throughout their lives.

In cold weather, the Comanche wore shirts made of deer, mountain sheep, or antelope hides. The skirts were often painted yellow or green.

Men, women, and children wore buffalo robes in the coldest weather. Men also wore fur-lined leggings.

Men wore their hair in long braids that they sometimes wrapped with fur or ribbons. They parted their hair in the middle. And they often painted the part red. If they were victorious in a hunt or warfare, men painted their faces black.

Men also wore earrings. Sometimes, they had 5 holes in their ear lobes for earrings. Men began to wear eagle feather war bonnets once they were confined to **reservations**.

Women wore their hair shorter than men. They painted their faces around their eyes with yellow or red. They made different colors from plants and clay.

A Comanche family in traditional dress

Crafts

The men made bows and arrows. It took great skill to make a bow. Most bows were made of strong, flexible wood from the Osage orange tree.

The wood was cut and scraped to the right size. After drying several months, the wood was greased with buffalo fat. Then it was wrapped with thin, wet strips of buffalo **tendon**. The tendon shrank as it dried. It made the wood strong and waterproof.

Bowstrings were made from several strips of tendon. They were twisted and held together with glue. The Comanche made glue by boiling buffalo horns and hooves.

Making arrows also required great skill. Each shaft had to be carefully crafted so the arrow could hit its target. Feathers were added to the shaft to make the arrow fly straight. An arrowhead was attached to the other end.

Comanche men also crafted shields from buffalo hide. Shields were important because they protected the warriors during warfare. The Comanche believed shields had magical power to protect them. A well-made shield could stop a bullet.

Sometimes, the men decorated their shields with **geometric** designs. A young warrior might ask an older warrior to share his shield design with him. A warrior might also get a design from images he saw in a dream or vision. Often, eagle or hawk feathers were tied to the shield.

An 1844 drawing of a Comanche chief with a spear, bow and arrows, and a decorated shield.

Family

When a Comanche man decided to marry, he had to complete a **vision quest** and take part in warfare.

Afterward, his family held a give-away to honor him. Then, he could marry. The man took a present of horses to the woman's family. If the family accepted the horses, and the man agreed to care for the woman's parents, the man and woman were married. Then, the woman moved into the man's tipi.

Long ago, Comanche men could have more than one wife. These extra wives were usually his first wife's sisters. The first wife had **authority** over the other wives. Sometimes, the extra wives were women who had been **widowed**.

Comanche families had few children. The parents, older children, uncles, and aunts raised each child. Boys moved into their own tipis when they became teenagers. Girls remained with their parents until they married, often at 13 or 14 years old.

A Comanche on
a vision quest

Children

When Comanche babies were born, they were washed and bundled in soft furs. Moss was used as a diaper. The babies were placed on a **cradleboard** for protection.

A Comanche cradleboard was made of a leather basket. It held the baby onto the backboard. Another leather covering was placed over the woven basket and attached to the board. This leather covering was decorated with **quill work** designs or, in later years, glass seed beads.

Babies slept between their parents at night until they were a year old. Children could have many names before they were given their adult name. The father usually named the baby. But sometimes, a friend was asked to name it during a **ceremony**.

Children were never spanked. If they misbehaved, their parents told them stories. The stories were told in a way that made the children understand proper behavior, and what was expected of them.

The grandparents helped raise the children. Mothers and fathers were usually busy. So, the grandparents had to take care of the children. They told their grandchildren stories. These stories taught them about the history and ways of their people. Children also learned by playing games that **imitated** adult roles.

A Comanche mother holds her child on a cradleboard

Myths

The Comanche used **myths** to explain nature. The following is the story of how the world was created.

§

The Comanche believed the Great Spirit created them from the dust swirls of a mighty storm. After humans were created, Earth shook with concern. It wondered how it was going to feed the people.

The Great Spirit thought about Earth's concern. The Great Spirit decided that Earth would feed humans physically during the day. At night, while they slept, the Great Spirit fed them **spiritually**. When the humans awoke in the morning, they felt spiritually full and renewed.

The Evil Spirit was cast out of the Spirit World after it refused to recognize humans as the Great Spirit's best creation. The Evil Spirit's punishment was to roam the earth forever.

The Evil Spirit began to trouble the people. It caused sickness, death, and hardship for them. Finally, the Great Spirit cast the Evil Spirit into a bottomless pit. But, the spirit hid in the fangs and stingers of poisonous creatures. The Comanche believe that the Evil Spirit continues to harm people to this day through these creatures.

The Great Spirit creates the Comanche in the swirls of a storm.

War

Once the Comanche moved to the plains, they were always at war. They defeated the Apache, Ute, Cherokee, Kickapoo, Shawnee, Delaware, and Caddo. They fought for the land and the buffalo herds. They also **raided** the Spanish settlements in Texas and Mexico and stole horses.

A Comanche war party was a terrifying sight. Warriors painted their faces red. They wore buffalo horns or eagle feathers tied in their hair. And they were experts with the bow and arrow, and rifle.

Some warriors carried lances and buffalo-hide shields. Lances were good for close fights. But, they were not good against an enemy with rifles. Lances were often decorated with feathers. The feathers shook in the wind and from the horses' movements.

The Comanche struck quickly. Then, they disappeared into the countryside. When cornered, the Comanche would fight to the death.

Not all warfare was violent. The Comanche also counted coup. Counting coup on one's enemy was dangerous, but it was rewarding. To count coup, a warrior had to ride into an enemy camp and touch a warrior with a stick.

To be touched by one's enemy was an insult. It meant that the enemy could have easily killed you. The person counting coup was well respected for his ability to get close to his enemy without killing him.

Comanche warriors with traditional weapons

Contact with Europeans

    Early in the 1700s, a Ute trading party brought other Native Americans to the Spanish settlements in New Mexico. The Spanish asked for the name of the other Native Americans. The Utes called them "Komantcia." That word meant "stranger," "enemy," or "someone who wants to fight us all the time."

    The Spaniards began to call these people "Comanche." So, too, did the American settlers. But, the Comanche called themselves the "Numinu" or "Nemene." It means "The People."

    The Comanche traded hides for European guns, knives, glass beads, kettles, cloth, and blankets. The Comanche traded with other tribes for horses.

Comanche trading with a European

Quanah Parker

Quanah Parker was the last chief of the Quahadi **band** of Comanche. He was the son of Chief Peta Nocona and Cynthia Ann Parker. Quanah Parker's mother was not a Native American.

When Cynthia Ann Parker was young, the Comanche captured her from her family's Texas farm. She grew to love her Comanche family. And, she chose to live with them.

On June 27, 1874, Quanah Parker led 700 braves in the battle of Adobe Walls. Adobe Walls was a trading post and fort in Texas. American buffalo hunters used the fort as a place to trade buffalo fur.

The Comanche and other Plains Indians disliked the buffalo hunters. The hunters threatened the buffalo herds. And they threatened the Plains Indians' way of life.

Quanah Parker was chosen during a **sun dance** to lead the war against the buffalo hunters. The Comanche, Cheyenne, and Kiowa fought hard. But, they were no match for the long-range rifles of the buffalo hunters.

Quanah Parker was the last of the Comanche war leaders to surrender to the U.S. Army. Until his surrender, he had never signed a **treaty** with the Americans. On June 2, 1875 Quanah Parker brought the Quahadi to the Indian **Reservation** in Oklahoma. He became a spokesman for his people because he could speak Spanish, English, and Comanche.

Quanah Parker

Parker also served as a judge on the Court of Indian Offenses. Quanah was considered to be a good judge. He used **traditional** Comanche ways of justice. For example, if a person stole a knife, the person would have to return it.

Quanah Parker had five wives and many children. He died on February 23, 1911.

The Comanche Today

In the Medicine Lodge **Treaty** of October 1865, the Comanche and the Kiowa gave up the southern part of their territory in central Texas to the U.S. government. The Comanche and the Kiowa kept much of western Texas and Oklahoma. It was set aside as a **reservation**.

In October 1867, the U.S. government broke the treaty promises and took this land. A new treaty was made between the U.S. government and the Comanche and Kiowa. The Comanche-Kiowa reservation was created in south-central Oklahoma. By 1907, the U.S. government had given each Comanche family 160 acres (65 ha) of poor farming land. During the rest of the 1900s, many Comanche left Oklahoma in search of a better life.

Today, around 8,500 Comanche live on the Comanche-Kiowa reservation. The Comanche are preserving their **traditional** ways by teaching its people the Comanche language.

Each year at the Cowtown Coliseum in Fort Worth, Texas, the Chisholm Trail Round-Up hosts the Quanah Parker Comanche **Pow-Wow** and Honor Dance. The event celebrates the rich history of the Comanche Nation. It also honors Comanche Chief Quanah Parker and his warriors' grand entry at the Coliseum's first indoor **rodeo** in 1918.

During the pow-wow, dancers from across the Southwest compete for prizes. This is one of the most popular and colorful of the Chisholm Trail Round-Up events. The performance of tribal dances and songs allows visitors to see some of the Comanche's **traditions** come to life.

Comanche also participate in the American Indian Exposition. It is held each year at the Caddo County Fairgrounds in Anadarko, Oklahoma. The Exposition gives native and non-native communities the opportunity to share the rich history, traditions,

Comanche in traditional dress perform a ceremonial dance called the Tuwee

and spirituality of Native Americans. It also allows them to enjoy a spirit of friendship and community.

The Exposition highlights the skills, talents, and experiences of individuals and tribes. And it encourages communication and business between the communities.

The Expo grand entry. The man on the left is dressed as a Comanche warrior did long ago.

Lanny Aseperme leads a horse for the 1999 Comanche Tribal Princess, Lanette Tachahwickah.

1998 Tribal Princess, Ellen Tahhahwah

Glossary

authority - the power to give commands and enforce orders.

band - a group of Comanche families who lived and moved together, a part of the larger group called the Comanche tribe.

breechcloth - a soft piece of hide or cloth, usually worn by men, that was wrapped between the legs and tied with a belt.

ceremony - a special act to be done on special occasions.

council - a group of people who meet, usually to make decisions.

cradleboard - a flat board used to hold a baby; it could be carried on the mother's back or hung from a tree so that the baby could see what was going on.

elder - a person having authority because of age or experience.

fringe - a border or trimming made of threads or cords, either loose or tied together in small bunches.

geometric - made up of straight lines, circles, and other simple shapes.

hemline - a border or edge on a garment.

imitate - to try to be like; to follow the example of.

myth - a legend or story that tries to explain nature.

poncho - a large piece of cloth or other material with a slit in the middle for the head to go through.

pow-wow - a ceremony of Native Americans, usually involving feasts, dancing, and performances.

quill work - the use of porcupine quills to make designs on clothing and cradleboards.

raid - a sudden attack.

reservation - land set aside by a treaty with the government for the home of a Native American tribe.

rodeo - a contest or exhibition of skill in roping cattle or riding horses and bulls.

sinew - a band of tough fibers that joins a muscle to a bone; also called tendon.

spiritual - sacred; religious.

sun dance - a sacred ceremony performed to show and give thanks. It is done to ask the Creator for renewal and protection of the people and the natural world.

tan - to make a hide into leather by soaking it in a special liquid.

tendon - a band of tough fibers that joins a muscle to a bone; also called sinew.

tradition - the handing down of beliefs, customs, and stories from parents to children.

travois - a simple vehicle used by Native Americans to move goods and people. A travois was made with two long tipi poles tied together to form a big triangle. Toward the bottom of the triangle, shorter poles were tied onto the tipi poles. The shorter poles formed a platform that carried food, children, and the elderly.

treaty - a formal agreement between nations.

vision quest - a way for Native Americans—especially young people—to communicate with nature and the spirit world. People on vision quests seek advice, answers to questions, and an understanding of why they have come to this earth.

widow - a woman whose husband is dead and who has not married again.

Web Sites

For information on the National Museum of the American Indian, see the Smithsonian's Web site: **http://www.si.edu/organiza/museums/amerind/abmus/index.htm**

Comanche Language and Cultural Preservation Committee:
http://www.skylands.net/users/tdeer/clcpc/

The American Indian Exposition Web site: **http://www.indianexpo.org/**

Maruawe! Welcome to Numuukahni/Comanche Lodge. This site is dedicated to the Comanche people: **http://members.tripod.com/~Quohadi/**

These sites are subject to change. Go to your favorite search engine and type in "Comanche" for more sites.

Index